STRATHINVER

A Portrait Album 1945-1953

STRATHINVER
A Portrait Album 1945-1953

Robin Bell

MACDONALD PUBLISHERS · EDINBURGH

ISBN 0 86334 035 0 (*cased*)
    0 86334 036 9 (*limp*)

Published by
Macdonald Publishers
Edgefield Road, Loanhead, Midlothian EH20 9SY

The publisher acknowledges the financial assistance of the Scottish Arts Council in the publication of this volume.

Printed in Scotland by
Macdonald Printers (Edinburgh) Limited
Edgefield Road, Loanhead, Midlothian EH20 9SY

Contents

Foreword, by Naomi Mitchison   9
Introductory Note   11

Prologue
One Day They Put Out The Flags   15

I
The Townfoot

Willie Barr, the Newsagent   21
Arthur Ritchie, the Electrician   22
Tony Stevens, the Ice-Cream Man   23
Jean Ross, the Telephonist   24
Jimmy Hood, the Garage Owner   25
Nancy Scott   26
Peter MacDonald, the Joiner and Undertaker   27
Donald Walker, the Watchmender   28
Dougal Morton, the Chimney Sweep   29
Stevie Wallace, the Barber   30
Adam Bruce, the Assistant Factor   31

II
The County Set

Roderick Milne, the Strathinver Estate Owner   37
Lady Lindley and her Companion, Miss Lawrie   38
Henry MacLeod, Major (Rtd) Scots Guards   39
Mrs Emily Harrison   40

Jamie Douglas   41
Brigadier Stanley   42
Old Mrs Murray of the Mill   43
Richard Hay, Son of Admiral Hay   44
Bertie and Alice McFadyen   45

III
The Churches

Reverend Peter Black, Minister of Strathinver Old Kirk   51
Mrs Catharine Black, the Minister's Wife   52
Gavin Black, the Minister's Grandson   53
David Constable, Senior Elder of Strathinver Old Kirk   54
Archie Simpson, the Beadle of Strathinver Old Kirk   55
Martha Buchan, Sunday School Leader of Strathinver
    Old Kirk   56
Reverend Neil Henderson, Minister of Strathinver West   57
Phyllis Hall, the Organist and Piano Teacher   58
Peter MacLean, Deacon of Strathinver West and Builder   59

IV
The School

Keir Matheson, Headmaster of Strathinver High School   65
Miss Watson, Primary One Teacher   66
Kate Cameron, Primary Three Teacher   67
Kirsty Gilmour   68
George Cairns, the Deaf Boy   69
Mary Clark   70
Liz Miller   71
Eric Young   72
Angela Carson   73

V
The Townhead

Walter Niven, the Butcher and Provost	79
Mrs Baxter of the Strathinver Arms	80
Davie Gordon, the Footballer	81
Oliver Campbell, the Lawyer	82
James Rollo, the Banker	83
Adam Mitchell, the Dentist	84
Russell Hume, the High-class Grocer	85
Cochrane, the Second-hand Bookseller	86
Dr Houston	87
Bella Thomson	88
Ben Morrison, the Roadman	89

VI
The Farms

George Armstrong, Strathinver Mains	95
Stuart Jamieson, the Crofter	96
Moira Weir, the Grieve's Wife	97
Sam Ryan, the Blacksmith	98
Sadie Gilfillan, the Dairy Farmer	99
Walter Shaw, the Shepherd	100
Eck Skinner, the Orraman	101
Sandy and Martha Craig, Tenant Farmers at Crossgate	102
Billy Gibb, the Ploughman	103
John Leslie, Tenant Farmer at Muirhead Farm	104

Foreword

Aberuthven was within walking distance of my own family home, Cloan on the slopes of the Ochils. Robin's post-war portraits and memories are of the forties and fifties, mine of the twenties—but yet, have folk changed that much? I seem to recognise them all, and maybe I could have met the wee boy from the Manse, a chiel among them making notes, seeing just that bit further through them than was maybe right and proper, setting them down in print. Surely some of them were Auchterarder rather than Aberuthven, most of all some of the pillars of the church, for here along the strath was the home of the Disruption.

This is middle Scotland with the Highlands staring down at us from the line of the Grampians along the north-western skyline. We are far enough from the bustling east coast, from the fishing harbours, as well as the big farms of the Mearns, still further from Glasgow, though we might make an occasional expedition to Edinburgh. Our speech is English but with a flavour of words and grammar that sets it apart from the southern sort. Robin has caught this fine in these portraits that stand up to be stared at, almost in the round.

NAOMI MITCHISON

Introductory Note

I was born in 1945 and grew up in the Manse of Aberuthven, a small village in central Perthshire where my father was the parish minister. Even to a small boy it was obvious that this was a period of great change. Although I did not realise it at the time, the outbreak of war in 1939 had temporarily suspended the building of new roads, houses and hydro-electric schemes. The war also made the farmers more conscious of agricultural efficiency even when neither fuel nor new machinery was readily available. It also accelerated the breakdown of the rural class structure so that when peace was declared in 1945 physical and social change came in a great rush.

Over the Manse hedges I could see tractors replacing Clydesdales. In the village, tarmac pavements and indoor plumbing did away with earth footpaths and the two village pumps. My parents were so glad to have electricity come at last that they threw out all our massive brass oil lamps. New houses were built and old ones repaired. I was able to go to school not long after my fourth birthday because there was a shortage of children but within a couple of years the two-roomed village school filled up with the post-war baby boom. I didn't ask why we stopped preserving eggs in isinglass or were suddenly able to get Mars bars more often, but I couldn't help noticing.

This period, important though it is to understanding how Scotland has come to be where it is today, tends to be forgotten between the saga of the Second World War and the brave new Elizabethan era of 1953. In *Strathinver* I have tried to convey what it was like to be part of a small rural community at that time. Paradoxically, it seemed more realistic to invent a new place than to reproduce an old one. I also found it necessary to devise a new narrative verse form to link the characters and let them come alive in their different ways.

I liked the place where I grew up, but the view from the Manse leaves no room for romantic illusions. I do not regret that the village has changed rapidly and generally for the better. Some things about the Scots temperament do not change much, however, and at least some of the characters in *Strathinver* are still alive and well today.

R. B.

Prologue

ONE DAY THEY PUT OUT THE FLAGS

The children in the town where no bombs dropped
believed in the war because the wireless news
kept on about it, and their mothers
mingled familiar names with others
who had once lived here. Believing made it true,
like knowing that time moved though the kirk clock stopped

and black-out curtains, sirens and sandbags
seemed to make sense. Eggs steeped in isinglass
sat in each kitchen of the long main street
in cupboards hungry for their monthly sweets.
Schooldays and summer holidays passed
peacefully. Then one day they put out the flags

and the whole town began to change once more.
The young men came back, wearing shoes not boots,
job hunting in utility jackets.
Their sweethearts dreamed of furniture dockets
and paint that was not green. At the Townfoot
the old folk said they'd seen it all before.

I

The Townfoot

WILLIE BARR
the Newsagent

The plump newsagent gossip, Willie Barr
begins his day with a mug of tarry tea
in the office of Stationmaster Bain,
waiting for the papers from the London train.
Bain listens, gets his *Glasgow Herald* free
and carries the bundles out to Willie's car

if asthma grips the newsagent's faded chest.
Twelve year old Ian, when his Dad returns,
loads up his bike while Willie puffs between
scribbling street numbers on *Scotsman, Bulletin,
Courier, Mail* and *Express* though Ian has learned
by heart which papers go to each address.

Down the long main street in the early light
with the news from the town foot to the Cross,
up by the granite villas on the Longmuir Road,
Ian pedals with his lightening load,
a trainee gossip never at a loss
for clues to embellish the previous night.

ARTHUR RITCHIE
the Electrician

He came here to cure his shattered nerves
and start a new life to replace the one
that died in the rubble of Clydebank.
Mills the ironmonger was the one to thank
who let him have the job his own dead son
should have come back to. Arthur Ritchie served

in the shop, filled oil cans, got to know
by reading catalogues the names of tools
of every kind though most were out of stock.
Gradually he got well, though he would talk
non-stop for half an hour then become cool
and silent. There was not enough to do

for two at the counter. Arthur began
to take on electrician's work once more,
though local power was just an evening dream
till they finished the giant hydro scheme;
but Arthur mended maid's bells and front doors
or sat and watched while acid bubbles ran

in charging batteries' thick green glass cells
for wireless sets that brought the Nuremberg news.
When pylons came, Arthur put electric light
into the big houses. Everything was bright,
but the congregation shivering in their pews
muttered, "The old oil lamps gave heat as well."

TONY STEVENS
the Ice-cream Man

Antonio Stefano changed his name
by tactful deed-poll when the war began
though he was born here and the only
Italian words he knew were "spumone"
and "tutti frutti." He gave up his van
to the Home Guard. Tony Stevens he became.

Somehow he still managed to make ice-cream
though it tasted quite different from before.
He eked out his tiny stock of wrapped sweets
with home-made toffee. For a Saturday treat
to top a vanilla cone Tony would pour
a little raspberry sauce and it would seem

the mothers really got their coupons' worth.
He was a ventriloquist and would pretend
that Donald Duck was hiding in the shop
and try to lure him out with acid drops,
liquorice strings or Mars bars. He would bend
long barley sugar twists and say the dearth

of sugar and business would soon pass.
He never seemed to be in a hurry
and could do conjuring tricks, but even he
when he heard his son was sent to Sicily,
though he said, "We can't let ourselves worry,"
went to the chapel each day to say Mass.

JEAN ROSS
the Telephonist

At home Jean Ross was just a quiet mouse
who scuttled round with dusters, cups of tea
and knitted bootees for the Sale of Work
while her one-armed husband did his best to shirk
any work at all. She listened patiently
while he trailed Goldflake smoke around the house

with puffs and sighs of Spitfire heroics
though he was just ground crew. To make ends meet
she got the job at the telephone exchange
and, out of the house, Jean Ross was changed
into a bright-voiced starlet. She would greet
each winking light by name. Her man was stoic

and went to tell his stories on the seat
in front of the Town Hall, but had to thole
old Doig on the Veldt and Ryan on the Marne
who had decades more practice with their yarns
while Jean's voice winged from telegraph pole to pole
with "Number please?" or "Would you please repeat?"

Her husband seemed to take it very hard
that she always knew just where the doctor was.
Urgent requests for house calls would get through
right away. She never let on she knew
of folk's affairs. The discretion of Jean Ross
concealed extra manoeuvres of the Home Guard.

JIMMY HOOD
the Garage Owner

Jim Hood arrived when petrol rationing went
and started off with two pumps and a shed.
When cars broke down there was no-one else but him.
He'd open the bonnet, rub his chin
and shake his long head. With the blacksmith's aid
he improvised new gaskets and unbent

track-rods, plugged balding tyres that farm roads burst.
Repairs came with an unwritten guarantee:
"If it doesn't go right, just bring it back."
He used piles of old bricks and motley jacks
to prop up cars and crawled beneath to see
while owners stood helpless, fearing the worst.

Jim Hood's real passion was detective books,
read with black thumbs upon his oily knees.
Seeing him sitting reading, bowed and lanky,
the minister called him "a detective manqué."
Jimmy laughed, though secretly he was pleased,
"A manky detective I would make."

But all this reading made Jim Hood equipped
to recognise dark stains, identify a car
and be star witness in a murder trial.
A legal nicety saved the men from jail.
Soon after Jim was found crushed in his yard.
The fiscal said it seemed a jack had slipped.

NANCY SCOTT

Respectable folk said Nancy Scott was "loose,"
seeming to overlook the obvious fact
that the bits of her that showed were much too tight.
Her clinging red sweater never quite
restrained her good points. Her belt was wide and black,
patent leather like her high-heeled shoes.

She was the star of local teenage dreams
and figured in middle-aged nightmares too,
for Nancy had a smile that seemed to show
just how well she knew you by her "Hello."
Peter Jones the draper denied he knew
where she got nylons with such perfect seams.

She didn't mind what the busy gossips said,
even enjoyed it, because it let her
make fun of prudes. She tried to be seen to flirt
with them, or greet couples, straightening her skirt,
with, "I hope your back is feeling better,"
and watch her face go white and his go red.

PETER MACDONALD
the Joiner and Undertaker

Each time he found his laddies wasting nails
he would punish them with the same old yarn
of how his namesake Grandad from the Isles
put no nails in coffins, but walked miles
to find good rowan dowels and cut down
his costs with shrouds made out of tattered sails.

"Why rowans?" the boys asked. "For the witches,"
said Peter with his heavy-lidded grin
and for a few minutes they would take more care
till they heard him go out to the pub to share
the silence of a half-pint with MacLean.
Then spooky mimes had all the boys in stitches.

Once one boy asked, "Would new-cut dowels not shrink
and let the planks get shoogled out of place?"
"How would you know what happens in the ground,"
growled Peter. "All Grandfather's lids stayed down."
The boys were too busy keeping a straight face
to hear his snort or see his sly half-wink.

When Peter himself died, they found his will
spelled out in detail all that should be done
to keep the business going, but no word
how the undertaker should be interred.
They made a box like any other one
but fixed his lid with nails and rowan dowels.

DONALD WALKER
the Watchmender

Donald was a school dux in Victoria's reign.
He became an accountant. At his desk
in London he watched the railways' long decline,
adding up LNER's struggling lines.
"There's no profit in being picturesque,"
he told the chairman again and again.

Nationalisation came as a release.
Donald worked out his pension and retired
to Strathinver to begin once more
the life he had left fifty years before.
He bought an old villa and sat by the fire
while his busy English wife never ceased

pottering in the steep herbaceous border.
One day as usual she brought in his tea
and found him lying sprawled upon his back,
blue-faced and gasping from a heart attack.
He lived. "Stop being so sedentary
or you'll die next time," Dr Houston ordered.

At first Donald went for long boring walks
then revived a hobby from his younger days
and mended watches. He inserted jewels
and balanced flywheels with his nimble tools.
Avoiding all other forms of exercise,
he lived for twenty years among his clocks.

DOUGAL MORTON
the Chimney Sweep

When you opened the door to Dougal Morton
he stood like the messenger of a modern god
in leather helmet, goggles and huge gloves.
He'd step back to eye the chimneys high above
then untie the ladders from the wobbly load
on the sidecar of his ancient Norton.

Dougal's coming was foreshadowed by the news
of previous days spread out before the hearth,
carpets rolled back and dustsheets everywhere.
He raised his bolted ladder in the air
and began his solemn ascent from earth
to battle with soot traps and blocked flues.

His dignified expression never cracked
even when he flexed his fuzzy-wuzzy brush
and held it at arm's length to check for kinks,
with his face like a school-boy spattered by ink.
His rumbling ball brought soot down with a rush
to billow the dark folds of his hopeful sack.

Dougal would stride back down the slippery slates
as if protected by an unseen hand.
He loaded up the ladders, brushes, sacks
into his wooden sidecar and rode back,
like a visitor from a half-mythical land
so foreign that he seemed appropriate.

STEVIE WALLACE
the Barber

The hamstrung bell that was supposed to ring
when you opened Stevie's outer door
rang only when you closed it once again
and hung up your coat and hat to let the rain
drip rhythmically on the brown linoleum floor
like faint applause for Benny Goodman's swing

from the bakelite radio's muted beat.
"It'll soon dry up. I'll not keep you waiting long,"
came Stevie's mirrored, optimistic smile.
*Saturday Evening Post*s in a neat pile,
sent by his brother, helped drown Sinatra's songs
and eased the waiting on his hard bench seat.

His barber's chair was a solid, wooden throne.
Small boys had to sit on a plank across its arms.
Steve would take a tousled profile and restore
the close-cropped symmetry of the month before,
then step back for perspective and for warmth
to the fire whose chimney echoed Crosby's groans.

When Stevie had electric light put in,
folk got used to the electric clippers' note.
Only Watt the policeman made him unplug,
"It's like a muckle wasp aboot ma lugs."
Huffy Steve shaped Watt's hair to make his ears stick out,
the better to hear Humphrey Lyttelton.

ADAM BRUCE
the Assistant Factor

The ploughman's son won a DFC and bar
but didn't talk about it, though he grew
a giant, ginger handlebar moustache
and at the Friday dances cut a dash
in blazer and squadron tie. The girls knew
that Adam Bruce was what wars were made for.

He came to his parents when he was demobbed.
"Your room is just as you left it," said his Mum.
Adam thanked her and changed it round himself
with new winged trophies on the mantleshelf.
He helped with the hay, brought the harvest home
and scanned the *Courier* for a proper job.

He nearly went to university
but assistant factor on the Milne Estate
suited him better and gave him a house,
a gatehouse with turrets that were no use
as rooms and an ivy-covered date
beneath the mock-Elizabethan chimneys.

It was a big house for an unmarried man
and no chance he could stay single there.
With his Air Force chest and ploughman's feet
he was the six month wonder of the main street
till Annie Watt won him by knowing where
the pilot ended and the plough began.

II

The County Set

RODERICK MILNE
the Strathinver Estate Owner

The Milnes had made their money out of jute
in Dundee, then engineering on the Clyde.
Old Angus bought the estate in World War One
when military contracts could be won
knee-deep in salmon rivers or in hides
where damascened twelve-bores would wait to shoot

capercailzies, pheasants and red grouse.
But young Roderick Milne's Lee Enfield on the Somme
was choked with yellow mud when he was gassed
and taken prisoner. When the First War passed
the bitterness stayed with the half-blind son
who lived on the Riviera till the house,

the estate, engineering works and cash
became his when old Angus finally died.
Roderick Milne would spend his summers here
then sail south for the rest of the year.
He sold the works that were his father's pride,
invested in the Rand and missed the Crash.

He was ready for the Second World War,
improved the house and lived here all the time.
His house parties did not fish or shoot or stalk,
but sat in the yellow drawing room and talked,
perched in Scotland in evening dress. When peace came,
like swallows they all fluttered south once more.

LADY LINDLEY
and her companion, Miss Lawrie

Miss Lawrie, in long white gloves and gingham frock,
dead-heads the floribundas patiently,
while Lady Lindley fills a wicker trug
with blooms for crystal vases and pale jugs,
secateurs in red scratched hands; her laddered knees
and tight replacement buttons on her smock

snag on the thorns. A dozen mismatched reds
are all she can find. "That will have to do,"
she says to her companion. "Where is Jock?
If you find his lead, I'll take him for a walk."
Miss Lawrie fetches, waits till her lady goes
then puts the garden tools back in the shed.

Lady Lindley's soles are thin, but the uppers
of her brogues gleam on the gravel drive.
She sees there are still some dead heads on the pinks,
calls Jock to heel, fastens his lead and thinks
Miss Lawrie is lucky to have a place to live.
Miss Lawrie wonders who will buy the supper.

HENRY MACLEOD
Major (Rtd) Scots Guards

Henry MacLeod had been a handsome man.
He had the Sandhurst manners, grey wavy hair,
soft voice and rather ponderous gait
of a man who'd almost been the welterweight
champion of the Army. He would wear
his heavy tweed suit in June and learned to stand

the heat more easily than his wife's sharp tongue.
Henry had no head for cash, nor had she
and never thought of buying their own home
till he retired and found the pension income
of a Major meant genteel poverty
and a dwindling social set to be among.

They rented a lonely farm-house near the moor
and kept a sad Alvis in the tin-roofed shed.
He liked to read library books, but got no peace
from his wife: "Do something, Henry!" He would ease
his tweedy bulk from the armchair, shake his head,
avoid her eye and amble to the door.

He went for long walks and took up studying plants
with the library's help. He brought home and dried
wild flowers and grasses, hedgerow leaves and moss.
His wife nagged, "Henry, you're a dead loss.
Why don't you find some mushrooms?" Henry tried
but accidentally cured his wife's complaints.

MRS EMILY HARRISON

Mrs Harrison on her dreadnought bike
looked like the Britannia on a penny
with swirling dress and peaked hat. Her sturdy wheels
seemed as protective as Britannia's shield.
Her voice was her trident. In full cry
she could pick off anyone she disliked

at two hundred yards. As county councillor
she had her beige-gloved hands in everything.
She raised funds to restore Strathinver Hall,
and put the new names on the War Memorial.
In the park she built new goalposts and swings
and repaired the bandstand's rotting floor.

The title, "royal borough" lapsed centuries before
but Mrs Harrison fought to win it back.
She sketched a new Strathinver coat of arms
to show the ancient hunt and modern farms.
She sent it to the Lyon who, with tact,
declined her "rampant sheep fretty and horns or."

She enlisted the help of Richard Hay
—Provost Niven did not want to be involved.
Learned letters flew, full of "bends engrailed,
chevrons, quarters, fess and pales."
As a tribute to Mrs Harrison, it was solved
by one booming horn and sheep's unwavering eyes.

JAMIE DOUGLAS

Scots born and English bred Jamie, in his teens,
had his first taste of New York and of jazz.
Barrymore, Fairbanks and the Prince of Wales
passed through his parties and he sometimes sailed
on the great white yachts "when sailing was
real sailing" before the coming of the *Queens*.

When his elder brother was shot dead in Spain,
fighting for the Loyalists, Jamie became heir
to family duty, not just family funds.
He never turned into an eldest son
but motored up and down to London where
in the nightclubs he could be a boy again.

His Alfa Romeo saved him from the war
by leaping from the road one drunken night.
His girl-friend died in flames. He was thrown clear
with a splintered jaw and torn left ear.
Deafness descended and the dancing lights
of London dimmed behind closed Mayfair doors.

Cold Scotland frightened him. The vanished heat
of jazz gave way for a while to muted tones
of clumsy landscapes painted in the hills.
Even these died. For three years he was ill,
listless with self-pity, till Cathy Jones,
the draper's shy girl, smiled at him in the street.

BRIGADIER STANLEY

When Brigadier Stanley and his wife came back
from their life in India, he was quite surprised
so little had changed while they were away.
Expecting improvements, he found slight decay.
The Times of India, he realised,
omitted Strathinver from its British map.

With Wavell he watched the old Raj's dying days,
at first with doubt and then with firm belief.
The Punjab slaughter shook him. He was sad
for broken Kashmir, fallen Hyderabad
and dead Gandhi, his awkward friend. His grief
was tempered by his trust in fair play.

In contrast Strathinver seemed, to him, dead set
against progress. He preached his Liberal views
with eloquent passion but with no success.
Gilfillan, the milkman, wished him all the best
but reminded, "They fowk would elect a coo
as long as it was wearing a blue rosette."

OLD MRS MURRAY OF THE MILL

Her square red house sat half-way up the hill,
frowning as the bungalows advanced.
Every morning Mrs Murray strode
down to the shops and back up with her load
of eggs, meat or fish—never all at once—
and lunched at the window where she saw the mill.

Her husband's partner, Jardine, ran it now
and with his mournful eyes said spinning wool
was not what it was. "It hasn't changed a bit,"
jabbed Mrs Murray with her hatpin wit.
"Money's still made by brains and lost by fools,"
adding more wrinkles to his bloodhound brow.

Her housekeeper, Nan Wilson, had a face
that loured beneath her old flapper's fringe and bob
and watched the mill fail while her employer,
as times worsened, vainly tried to annoy her
by needling Jardine with, "At least Nan knows *her* job.
She does what she's paid for, aye, and knows her place."

RICHARD HAY
Son of Admiral Hay

Jutland and Jellicoe made Richard's Dad
who became a peace-time admiral and retired
to Bournemouth before the Second War began.
Richard rarely saw the lean old man
who disliked him. "You never saw a shot fired,"
growled the admiral when his gout was bad.

Father and son looked alike, but had
nothing else in common with each other.
In Nineteen Twenty, when Dad was at sea,
the 'flu epidemic hit his family.
Richard lost his Mum and older brother
and was sent to the only aunt he had,

the Strathinver pony breeder, Janet Hay.
He went to boarding school, worked in her stables
in the holidays, till he caught TB
at fourteen. He went to Switzerland where he,
in the pallid breathless days, was able
to study French and Scottish history.

He married Aunt Janet's assistant, Clare
who managed the stables while Richard wrote
magazine features on Celtic folklore,
far from his father. But when he opened the door
of his wardrobe, one day, his shoes and coats
smelled like the admiral's and made him gasp for air.

BERTIE AND ALICE McFADYEN

The McFadyens bought up Glasgow tenements,
let them and their tenants rot then sold the sites
for council houses. They left town and let
their Kelvinside home to join the county set.
They bought old Cairncross Lodge but never quite,
despite all the money that they spent,

became accepted in their chosen land.
Bertie McFadyen joined the syndicate
of Curlett the game dealer but always seemed
to shoot at the point where pheasants had just been.
His wife, Alice, wanted to redecorate
the Lodge, but could not understand

what Gilmour the tactful painter had to say
about how tastes had changed. She went ahead
with her plans but redid it completely
when Mrs Hay, who finally came to tea,
said that the Festival of Britain made
"houses like ours look positively decayed."

She placed her generous offerings in the Kirk plate
and waited to be truly recognised.
Once when neither Lady Lindley, nor Miss Hay,
nor any of the Milnes could be free on the day,
she was asked to give the Sunday School prizes.
Bertie, in thanks, paid for new Kirk roof slates.

III

The Churches

REVEREND PETER BLACK
Minister of Strathinver Old Kirk

The Reverend Peter Black was dazzling white,
a chubby albino with fleecy hair.
Inducted to his charge in 1910,
he shared his jubilee with King George and then
settled down with the same sermons, hymns and prayers
for another twenty-five rounds of the good fight.

At first his parish called him "the wee lamb of God"
for his woolly hair and innocent face
and the name stuck, though Peter Black grew up
from a lamb to a wily, tough old tup.
He knew how to manipulate country ways
and ruled his kirk session with an iron rod.

He believed in visiting each of his flock.
The sight of his precarious black hat
and long black coat approaching the front gate
made even the county set sit up straight;
but once inside he'd chat and stroke the cat
and then sit back and listen to their talk.

When one of his deacons, Colin Wood, was caught,
drunk in his car, the elders said he should resign.
But Peter Black poured him one dram at the manse,
dressed him down and gave him a second chance.
"Thanks, Mr Black," said Wood, "I'll not let you down."
Old Peter banged down his glass, "You'd better not!"

MRS CATHARINE BLACK
the Minister's Wife

With her tweeds and twinsets Mrs Catharine Black
looked fresh from the pages of *Country Life*
but, like her husband, she was down-to-earth.
She'd reduce the Women's Guild to helpless mirth
with pawky stories but, as the minister's wife,
still keep her dignity. She had the knack

of disarming people with an easy grace.
She talked on equal terms to the county set
who remembered her mother—as well they might—
the roly-poly dragon, Lady Wright.
She knew everyone and would not forget
the family history behind each face.

At Harvest Thanksgiving she was at her best.
She'd challenge proud gardeners the previous week,
"Surely your carrots can't be as good this year?",
then wait for prize specimens to appear,
cannonball onions, huge swedes, wrist-thick leeks,
and welcome them, suitably impressed.

The choir sang, "All good gifts are sent from heaven,"
surrounded by dahlias and pots of jam.
When the decorations came down again,
the pulpit sheaves went to Mrs Black's hens.
The rest she parcelled for the sick, the "Home,"
a cornucopia in her Austin Seven.

GAVIN BLACK
the Minister's Grandson

In '43 Gavin came to the manse,
an owlish evacuee from the blitz,
making his grandparents parents once again.
Only the three-storey patterned wall remained
of his Chiswick house after a direct hit.
His sleeping parents never stood a chance.

He sat in the smouldering basement with his bear
waiting, like a good boy, for rescuers to come.
They cuddled him, gave him tea and sent him here.
He never cried; his Grandmother shed the tears.
He seemed to accept that his Dad and Mum
had gone to heaven and were happy there.

He did well at school but liked to play alone
in the rambling sheds and gardens of the manse.
Peter Black asked no local boys in to play
and Gavin preferred grown-ups anyway,
like Tony Stevens and especially Vic Lanz,
the Polish pilot who drove Niven's van.

Gavin made up stories, sometimes wrote them down,
careful structures, half-fantasy, half-truth.
The Old Kirk's congregation never knew
that they were spies and spacemen. Gavin grew
at a tangent to the rest, a slim, shy youth,
a fourth person singular for the town.

DAVID CONSTABLE
Senior Elder of Strathinver Old Kirk

Each Sunday morning two elders would wait
inside the kirk door by a small oak table
to greet folk as they climbed the wide stone stair,
taking note of who was or was not there,
welcoming visitors and, if they were able,
counting what they dropped into the plate.

David Constable was senior to them all,
a retired saddler who still smelled of leather
except in his Sunday clothes. He knew just how
the church finances stood, though Willie Gow,
the gloomy baker, was the treasurer.
"I don't see how we can get by at all,"

Gow would say to worry the kirk session,
tapping the ledger with his fountain pen.
Constable would catch the minister's eye
who would pray for assistance from on high
and end the meeting. Constable remained
to give the minister the real position.

When the farmers, who never were big spenders,
cut their seasonal yield, Constable had a word
with the minister who would say, "Next week,
Mr Constable, I'll just have to preach
my sermon about Caesar and the Lord
and what these auld skinflints should render."

ARCHIE SIMPSON
the Beadle of Strathinver Old Kirk

No-one remembered just how long it was
since Archie became beadle at the Kirk,
but it was even before Peter Black.
A tiny man, with silver hair slicked back,
he bore the bible, made the heating work,
solemnly rang the bell and mowed the grass.

His cleft palate made him hard to understand
but he made use of his impediment.
When people spoke to Archie, he'd reply
with a negative shake and a loud "Aye."
Rather than struggle to find out what he meant,
they'd let him get on with his ploys and plans.

He was a keen fisherman and caught,
in the Estate burns, trout fat as speckled stones.
Old Angus Milne had somehow let him fish
and no-one liked to stop him going where he wished.
Young Roderick thought of him as a garden gnome
but never knew whose trout the housekeeper bought.

MARTHA BUCHAN
Sunday School Leader of Strathinver Old Kirk

Martha Buchan had six children of her own
and fourteen grandchildren. She needed more
and clucked over the Sunday School like a hen
with new chicks. When she sang out the last amen
and the children scuttled for the door
it seemed an age till Sunday would come round again.

The children learned their texts and squeaked their hymns.
Jesus and Martha Buchan made them shine
with a clear, clear light till they knew off by heart
the flannelboard sagas of Noah's Ark,
Samson, Goliath, Samuel, Gadarene swine,
and could tell cherubim from seraphim.

She especially loved the Good Samaritan
and gave many of them an early start.
When they grew up and wed, it was her goal
to encourage them to swell the cradle roll.
Unblushing brides turned pink when, pure of heart,
Martha advised, "Do it as soon as you can."

REVEREND NEIL HENDERSON
Minister of Strathinver West

The congregation of Strathinver West
agreed, with ill-grace, in 1929,
to Church reunion rather than be
classed with UF (Continuing) or Wee Free.
Ministers stayed only five years at a time
then found a parish where they were less stressed

by muddled feuds and touchy deacons' courts.
In '48 Neil Henderson arrived.
Mrs Murray sniffed, "He's just a city wean.
Mind what I say: he'll soon gang back again."
He and his scholarly young wife survived
only a few months before there were reports

that he proposed new hymns to the church choir,
was thinking of a youth club and, worst of all,
that he had been to tea with Father Burke.
In his speech of thanks at the Sale of Work
he forgot to mention Phyllis Hall,
but said more funds were needed for the spire.

Mrs Henderson was struck completely dumb
by the constant need for compromise and tact.
Her nerves began to go and she was filled
with dread of the Rural and the Women's Guild,
but they lasted five years before going back
to the peace and quiet of the Glasgow slums.

PHYLLIS HALL
the Organist and Piano Teacher

It was said that a sailor jilted Phyllis Hall
then her next love, an airman, was shot down.
Only the army was left and she tried hard
to capture Captain Stewart of the Home Guard,
but only after he suddenly left town
did she find out he did not want girls at all.

She never took another risk, but tracked
the men of Strathinver with her narrowing eyes.
Every errant husband, ardent son
suspected Phyllis Hall knew what went on.
By arching an eyebrow she could imply
lewd practices and unspeakable acts.

As unpaid organist in Strathinver West
each Sunday morning she would face the choir,
peering over her music at the faces
of gigolo tenors, lusty basses
who came, she imagined, only to admire
how singing swelled the sopranos' chests.

She held a private piano class
twice a week, girls only, at her home.
She offered individual lessons too
but those who could, or would, afford them were few.
Angela Carson was the last to come.
She noticed drawn curtains and a smell of gas.

PETER MACLEAN
Deacon of Strathinver West and Builder

Peter MacLean's bite was much worse than his bark.
He never spoke except to contradict.
Silent in blue serge at the Deacons' Court
he'd sit, then shake his long moustache and snort,
"It's just not right!" His heavy walking stick
made a dotted line across the park

while his bandy legs bore him to the fray
with a mind as rigid as a bulldog's jaw.
He would argue about anything.
"It was only decent to toll for the King,"
he said, but that did not mean he saw
that bells should be rung on Coronation Day.

"But the bells would be a loyal greeting
to the young Queen," said Mr Henderson.
MacLean reached out as if to beckon,
"Is she Liz the First or Liz the Second?"
and sat back squarely, knowing he had won
though it was postponed till the next meeting.

IV

The School

KEIR MATHESON
Headmaster of Strathinver High School

His great patrician nose served to remind
that we were honoured to have Keir Matheson
as Head of Strathinver High, or so he thought.
He came here from Edinburgh and taught
as a latter-day muscular Christian,
with wide-open windows and closed mind.

During the war years, he looked on with gloom
while the school roll fell and no babies were born.
Despite his beliefs, he felt it an outrage
to shrink his personal empire and prestige.
When the soldier sweethearts finally returned,
his chest inflated with the baby boom.

He seldom bothered with the Primary School
but watched the Secondary girls and boys
with his eagle eyes. If any child did wrong
they were sent to face the Head's Lochgelly thongs
which fell from his heavens with a hissing noise.
"To be kind, one sometimes must be cruel,"

was one of the proverbs which he scattered
to help the school cultivate his moral code.
Prompt before dinner, he'd say, every night,
"The children don't respond as well as they might."
His wife, Eunice, would sympathise with, "I know,"
and pour dry sherry for his troubled waters.

MISS WATSON
Primary One Teacher

From the five-year-olds' very first school bell
Miss Watson had her priorities right:
first they learned to sit still with fresh-washed faces;
next they straightened socks and tied their laces.
Once they learned manners, they could learn to write
fat rounded letters, then count, read and spell.

The Head said she should "break the children in.
Prepare them for Parnassus' lower slopes."
After twenty years it still amazed her
that they should grow to fit their outsize blazers,
as rulers and rubbers replaced combs and soap
and earnest expressions grew from glaikit grins.

Miss Watson was trim. Miss Watson was precise.
Her little shadow stalked them all their days.
Raucous Fifth Formers fell silent when addressed
by their first teacher, who stared them in the chest
till they shrank to her size to hear her say,
"I do not think that was very nice."

KATE CAMERON
Primary Three Teacher

Kate Cameron came here at twenty-four,
the youngest teacher since the school began.
The Head took to her because of her good degree
and no male applicants for Primary Three.
She kept order by making lessons fun,
a method which had not been tried before.

Kate was a country girl from Forfarshire.
She studied at St Andrews, trained in Dundee
and that was all the Headmaster knew
or cared to know. One day the Queen passed through
on her way north. The school turned out to see
and when the long black car slowed down they cheered.

The car stopped. The Head stepped forward, but the Queen
called, "Kate, have you forgotten us so soon
at Glamis? When are you going to come?"
Kate blushed, "Perhaps in the summer holidays, Ma'am."
"I hope so," said the Queen. The car drove on
past the gaping Head and joyous Primary Three.

KIRSTY GILMOUR

Her Mum ran off with an accordion player
leaving ten year old Kirsty to keep house
for her painter father. She had his tidy ways
that helped to drive her scatty Mum away.
She did the cooking and her Dad got used
to lighting the fire and having, as his share

of the dusting, everything above four feet.
He encouraged Kirsty's work at school.
At night, instead of arguing with her Mum,
Gilmour could help Kirsty with her sums.
He made her left-handed letters stand up tall
and heard the tables she had to repeat.

The well-meaning minister, Neil Henderson,
praised Gilmour but said Kirsty should have more fun
and not just work. "Aye, well. On Saturday,"
said Gilmour, "she could go to the matinee
at the Regal." So, at half past one,
Kirsty fell in love with Errol Flynn.

It was only a trailer, but it was enough.
Kirsty grew old and young at the same time
in the faded velvet of the threepenny rows.
When the swirling curtains finally closed
the music stayed with her. She thought of her Mum
and wiped her eyes dry with her school blouse cuff.

GEORGE CAIRNS
the Deaf Boy

No-one realised that George Cairns was deaf
till he went to school. By then it was too late.
Dismissed as stupid for his first five years,
George angrily acted out his family's fears
with animal noises and eyes filled with hate.
He perfected a low, braying laugh

which he knew distressed his nervous Mum.
He'd embarrass her in their greengrocer's shop
just by being there. "There's no insanity,"
she'd insist, "on my side of the family."
His patient father tried to help her cope
but had no time left for his scowling son.

When George got a deaf aid words rushed in,
upsetting the way he saw himself.
Others' ideas flowed through his flood gates.
He learned quickly, could be articulate,
then sullenly nudge boxes off a shelf
and watch the apples bruise with his gaping grin.

One day he saw Miss Muir with her pail outside,
hirpling from the pump back to her flat,
one of the last without an inside tap.
George asked gruffly if he could take it up.
She gave him the pail. "You're a thoughfu' lad."
George brought her water each day till she died.

MARY CLARK

She was the quiet one who held the rope
for others to skip. She had no special friends
but was picked early in the playground games,
and it was always Mary Clark who came
when there were bumped heads or grazed knees to mend.
She seemed to take it on herself to cope

with others' crises. "She should be a nurse
when she grows up," her Girl Guide leaders said,
and for a while it seemed they would be right;
but something happened to her on the night
of her fifteenth birthday. Rumours spread.
Some said she got drunk or sick or worse.

She was seen at the doctor's. People said
she must be pregnant, but she grew more thin
and suddenly left school and went away.
"She's found a job down south," her Mum would say.
Her stepfather would just nod and grin
and scratch the eyebrows on his pale round head.

LIZ MILLER

Liz Miller was impossible to tig.
She was yards faster than the other girls
and ducked the boys' lunges with a neat sidestep.
At the Primary School Sports she sprinted, leapt
and ran the relay with long legs that whirled
as though she rode on an invisible bike.

As she grew older she won every race
for her age group and stayed till the Fifth Form,
enduring Highers so that she could compete
in the National Championships for school athletes.
The gangling redhead would arouse the scorn
of public school coaches for her awkwardness

in limbering up and her dislike of blocks.
They changed their minds when the starting pistol fired.
Liz's skinny chest would break the tape
before other girls could accelerate.
When her school days ended she retired
from running but, four years later, for a joke,

Liz entered the hundred at the Strathinver Games.
She shot into the lead but slipped and fell
and sat laughing till she was hauled to her feet
by the junior heavyweight, Nicol Reid
whose father owned the County Park Hotel.
He carried her off and, next year, changed her name.

ERIC YOUNG

Eric, like the first swallow of spring,
was always first to bring in a new season
of marbles or conkers to the playground.
Instinctively, as the year rolled round
and water pistols gave way with no reason
to catapults, Eric would be first to bring

a new one or an old one from last year.
Within a fortnight all the other boys
would have the same by nagging their parents
for extra pocket money to be spent
at the small glass counter crammed with toys
by the wheezing newsagent, Willie Barr.

When Eric first appeared with braces on his teeth
big Dougan jeered, "Whit's thon scrapyard in yer face?"
Eric pointed skywards with a grin.
Dougan looked up. Eric kicked him in the shins.
Then off to the staff-room window Eric raced
and innocently played hop-scotch underneath.

You could tell the war was over when tommies
turned into spacemen. Rommel became Sitting Bull
and Eric, the French Foreign Legionnaire,
volleyed snowballs through the desert air.
He died at nineteen in a real jungle,
facing a new enemy, the Commies.

ANGELA CARSON

Angela Carson was a blue eyed blonde
in a town of dark hair and hazel eyes.
Her father was killed in France when she was four
and her mother, though she'd never worked before,
opened a shop that sold gloves, scarves and ties
and said she worked her fingers to the bone.

Mrs Carson would sometimes buy bolt ends
of pre-war cloth and make a tailored skirt
with ample seams to let it out or in
and in the back shop, tight lips clasping pins,
perform slow fittings till her sharp knees hurt
while clients sniffed, "It seems a lot to spend."

Angela took piano, country dance
and spoke nicely in earshot of her Mum.
She won a bursary to a private school
and was made to stay though other girls were cruel.
They all did things her Mum said were "not done,"
told lies and swore and stole if they'd the chance.

She sensed that she was out of place, absurd,
but just to please her Mum she kept on trying.
She was good at sums and spelling, even dates
but she couldn't keep popular songs straight.
She'd come home with a good report card, crying
because she'd muddled Johnny Ray's sweet words.

V

The Townhead

WALTER NIVEN
the Butcher and Provost

Nothing was expected of town councillors
and they confirmed the voters' expectation.
The names of the councillors seldom changed
and Provost Niven kept the big gilt chain,
not through intrigue but because he was the one
with a chest more impressive than the others.

He was a huge man with red hands
that tucked a side of beef under one arm.
In his shop only the best was good enough
for his fillet steak, mince or potted hough.
His brother, Alec, ran their cattle farm
with a gold-scrolled W & A Niven on their van.

For years the provost's lamps shone at his gate.
His chain of office seemed like a watch chain;
the great medallions shrank against his girth.
His term revolved as surely as the earth.
His speeches were short. His invoices were plain.
He kept up his prices and kept down the rates.

MRS BAXTER
of the Strathinver Arms

Jessie Baxter kept the Strathinver Arms.
With her tight grey bun, long nose and steel-rimmed specs
she looked like a storybook schoolma'm
but she measured out a generous dram
when she was smiled at. She was easily vexed
by muddy boots or collies from the farms

that sprawled on the hearth and let no-one get near.
She had two rooms upstairs where salesmen stayed
or young couples called Smith would pass the night.
She could sense the early warnings of a fight
and Jessie's "Nae mair o' that" would be obeyed
with just a sullen shuffle or a sneer.

Her fat son, Billy, when he was in his teens
was made to help, but never at the bar.
He'd sign young couples into the hotel book
then listen at their wall or try to look,
crouching on the flat kitchen roof's cracked tar,
for glimpses to feed his overnourished dreams.

DAVIE GORDON
the Footballer

Davie Gordon thundered a late goal
from thirty yards to win the League Cup
and the part-time wing-half suddenly,
the papers said, was worth a big transfer fee.
Hibs and Rangers watched him, then a London club
moved quickly and he found he had been sold

into the English First Division.
His new club played him as a centre-forward
but Davie could not keep cool when he was kicked,
lashed back and got sent off. He was easily tricked
by shrewd defenders and seldom scored
or looked like scoring. The crowd's derision

worsened his temper and his clumsy fouls.
He went down to a Second Division club
and, back at wing-half, looked a different man
till he broke a forward's leg and was banned
for two months. He retreated to the pub,
missed training and, as a full-back, was sold

to a Third Division (North) side in decline.
One day a raw winger with a fancy swerve
was tripped. The winger got up and swung a boot,
ending Davie's career with a shattered foot.
Some Strathinver folk said, "That's what he deserved."
Others gave sympathy while he bought them pints.

OLIVER CAMPBELL
the Lawyer

Oliver Campbell was a clever man
with nothing to do but conveyancing and wills,
all drafted by Miss Carlyle, his clerk.
He drank his lunch in the County Park
with Harvey the chemist then showed off his skills
on the golf course till it was club house time again.

He spent week-ends at his Edinburgh club.
He was well-known to the girls of Danube Street
who listened while he bewailed his rural fate.
On their stairs he made way for advocates
whom he recognised but could not greet.
He dropped dead at fifty in a Rose Street pub.

Peter MacDonald watched while his laddies dug
the lawyer's grave in Strathinver kirk yard.
One lad said, peching, "It's an awfu' shame
he deed the way he did wi' a' his brains."
MacDonald looked askance. "It's not all that sad.
He's a Campbell. What do you expect?" he shrugged.

JAMES ROLLO
the Banker

James Rollo—never Jimmy—kept his desk
free from paper so the mahogany
and inset, red-tooled-leather surface gleamed,
under the Art Nouveau inkstand that seemed,
like its custodian, to embody
solidity with just a hint of risk.

In Rollo's inner sanctum he'd take tea
with favoured customers and give advice
in the rosy glow of the *Financial Times*.
He would proffer some dense documents to be signed,
then countersign in his own hand, precise
and rounded as his name. At five to three,

he'd nod to Miss Forbes to close the double door.
She'd bolt one half, leave the other ajar
for anyone who dared to rush in so late.
Lateness was something he'd not tolerate
unless the latecomer came in a big car
and strode, unsmiling, across his marble floor.

He believed that only rich folk had a right
to be in debt and tried to make an example
of poor Miss Muir, but enraged "the Lamb of God," who
transfixed smug Rollo on Sunday in his pew
with "The Moneychangers in the Temple"
followed next Sunday by "The Widow's Mite."

ADAM MITCHELL
the Dentist

Adam Mitchell spent a dreary war
in Edinburgh checking new recruits.
He patched them up and passed them one by one
with gleaming incisors to face the Hun.
Making one lot of strangers fit to shoot
at other strangers made no sense any more

after the first few hundred bared their teeth,
but to keep on was easier than to stop.
He married Minnie Gow when she was a nurse
and returned to Strathinver in due course
to start a practice over her Dad's shop
while Willie Gow sold bread and rolls beneath,

sighing, "He'll never make a living here."
The end of sweetie rationing helped his trade
so did the coming of the National Health.
Adam aspired to no great status or wealth,
bought a new bungalow by the mill lade,
got used to Minnie's demanding, "Adam, dear."

Amiable inertia kept him there
but he grew thin. Cancer was diagnosed.
He had to stop work and lay in his bed
listening, while in the sitting-room Willie said,
"He's lasting longer than I would have supposed."
Minnie snapped, "He might have taken better care."

RUSSELL HUME
the High-Class Grocer

Like his founding father, Russell Hume
was a portly barometer of esteem.
The higher your standing on the social grade,
the longer you could leave his bills unpaid.
Only the poor went where the brass till gleamed
in his scented shop's cathedral gloom.

His three assistants, dressed in long green coats,
dispensed hushed good taste to the waiting queue.
Hume would only emerge from the back room
to apologise for post-war prunes
or rush to help with, "Good morning, how are you?"
when Miss Lawrie, with her vaguely scribbled note,

turned the handle the wrong way on the door.
On Thursday afternoons the phone would ring
in the big houses so that Hume could send
precisely wrapped orders for the week-end.
When he finally asked, "Will that be everything?"
he made you think of several items more.

He kept lidded tubs of oatmeal, lentils, peas
beside tea cannisters and a machine to grind
your mutual choice of coffee beans.
His manner made his bacon seem more lean.
His business and his sugar were refined
and his wire slid smoothly through the yellow cheese.

COCHRANE
the Second-hand Bookseller

The wind drops and the weary rain clouds wait
to drizzle down on Cochrane's sixpenny shelves.
He opens the door, sticks out his mild, bald head
then drags his green tarpaulins out to spread
on drowsy novels. Poems can fend for themselves
while Cochrane stirs the cinders in the grate

and thinks about another pail of coal.
The draught beneath the faded blue front door
stirs thin dust on the walls he means to paint.
Bibles from silent pulpits, lives of saints
doze in precarious heaps upon the floor
while Cochrane dances to keep out the cold.

"Improving literature" is mixed with tales
by gentlemen travellers who record
foreign discomforts with the eye of Empire.
Cochrane gives in and puts coal on the fire.
He sits there silent with a million words,
framed by stags at bay, dark hills and billowing sails.

A customer comes in. Cochrane makes haste
to close the door and save the pretend heat,
then sits beside the tantalising box
marked "not for sale," pulls up his long wool socks,
rubs his thin thighs and drums his frozen feet
while old school prizes await a change of taste.

Dr HOUSTON

Dr Houston, brusque and bald, would skip
two stairs at a time to patients in their beds.
Nimble as a varsity three-quarter,
he'd tackle Strathinver's sons and daughters.
Thermometer poised, he'd hear half what they said,
shake the mercury and thrust it in their lips.

His cures were simple: exercise or rest;
liquid expectorants or laxative pills.
It worked. For he was called, nine times out of ten,
to ease the stomach, dry up the phlegm
or just reassure. But if a child fell ill
he'd take great care and pay for hospital tests.

Stupidity would make him sarcastic.
When mothers of four with an ominous swelling
would finally organise themselves to come
and ask him what they were suffering from,
he'd growl back, "You should need no telling:
it's weakness of the knicker elastic."

From time to time he courted Charlotte Hay
who lived in Hove but came to see her cousins.
Other girls would come with chest complaints and hope
but he chilled their ardour with his stethoscope.
He married Charlotte. Presents came in dozens,
like wishful kisses on his wedding day.

BELLA THOMSON

Even when there were no cats to be heard,
which was not often, you could always find
old Bella Thomson's cottage by the scent
of ginger toms and souring milk. She was bent
nearly double as though she had been designed
for reaching down to smooth out ruffled fur.

She never liked to hear of kittens drowned
though there were far too many on the farms,
and it was strange how Bella Thomson knew
when litters in distant steadings were due.
She would confront a farmer in his own barn
and make him say she could keep each one she found.

Her cottage had no curtains. It was damp
and she hardly ever lit a fire.
All her money was spent on milk and scraps.
Even indoors she wore a coat and hat.
After complaints, she locked in "Bella's choir"
each night before she blew out her oil lamp.

The lamp was seen to burn too late for her
one February night and then a sound
of crackling and hissing trickled through the thatch.
Men going home from the pub could only watch
while even the dry grass by the dyke around
gave off the lonely scent of burning fur.

BEN MORRISON
the Roadman

Of all the seasons, spring he liked the least
when he was made to join the tarry squad,
patching the winter's ragged ruts and cracks.
While others chatted, Ben would turn his back
and press on with the mending of the road
till the foreman said that he could be released

to work by himself on his favourite stretch
of the main road from Strathinver through the glen.
For three seasons he would scythe the verges
then take his heuk and trim the hedges.
He'd finish one side, cross the road again
and work his way back. He cleared the ditches

to let the camber drain away the spate.
The foreman knew better than to interfere
or check up on how he spent his time.
Ben would just growl, "Can ye no see I'm daein fine?"
When surveyors for the road-widening scheme appeared
he glowered at their white hands and theodolites.

One summer morning shy Richard Hay saw Ben
and made an awkward joke about General Wade.
"Aye," said Ben. "Thon man kent a thing or two,
but he hadnae the sense tae leave room for the snow."
"Telford did though," said Hay. Both men stood amazed
to recognise both knowledge and a friend.

VI

The Farms

GEORGE ARMSTRONG
Strathinver Mains

George Armstrong farmed—and owned—Strathinver Mains
and bought two other farms. He had three sons,
all of them careful copies of their Dad.
At the market he'd mutter, "Not too bad,"
as the weighbridge creaked beneath his record tons
of barley for the maltings. He'd complain,

no matter whether it was wet or dry,
and listen to the forecast with distrust.
He did his sums and found it not too hard
to send his Clydesdales to the knackers' yard
in favour of tractors: "Aye, needs must.
Ye can't afford to let time pass ye by."

He had no time for the county set,
though Mrs Armstrong took the *Scottish Field*
and read it on the new moquette settee
between the preparing of the ample tea
and Armstrong's coming back in from the fields
with "I'd like to see the lambs just fatter yet."

He used a sharp accountant, grudged the price,
but drummed it into his sons that it made sense
to pay for legal or financial fees
to lower the tax or raise the subsidies.
He'd cock his head, "It's no coincidence
the best folk get a' the best advice."

STUART JAMIESON
the Crofter

Stuart Jamieson had good ideas and cash,
but never had both of them at once.
His best schemes were never put to the test
because he had no money to invest.
Or, when his small savings gave him the chance
to back an idea, he'd no ideas to back.

He owned a little farm, more like a croft,
and never settled down to one main crop
but switched from pigs to raspberries, sugar beet
to brussels sprouts. He never could compete
with more established growers and had to stop.
He'd think up a new plan in the hayloft

where he liked to sit and churn his brain all day.
He and his frugal wife made do for years,
while he foresaw combines, chain stores, frozen food,
but none of it did him any good.
When he died his wife had the best idea:
renting the fields to Armstrong who could make them pay.

MOIRA WEIR
the Grieve's Wife

Big Andrew Weir was Armstrong's blunt-nosed grieve,
well-spoken at the farmhouse, but uncouth
and sharp-tongued with the men around the steading.
Folk pitied his bride, Moira, at their wedding,
for Andrew's temper, crudeness, gibes and drouth
were legend. His own mother believed

that skinny, innocent Moira would be hurt.
But Andrew came back from his honeymoon week
with the face of a spoilt brat who'd had the belt
for the first time. He made his presence felt
even more harshly at work, but he turned meek
at five o'clock, trudged home and kept the dirt

from his boots, as she said, "off my nice clean steps,"
though she deferred to him in front of other men.
Moira Weir's tidy life was organised
with a method and timing as precise
as the tiny handfuls that she fed the hens
or the spotless linoleum that she swept.

When Andrew broke his leg, wee Moira walked
to Armstrong's house to see about the pay.
"It was his fault," said Armstrong. "Is that a fact?"
she snapped, "You should know fine the farm safety act."
That evening, in hospital, she came to say,
"Mr Armstrong kindly agrees you'll not be docked."

SAM RYAN
the Blacksmith

Sam Ryan viewed machinery with contempt.
Anything more complex than a harrow
would lie in his back yard for days on end
unless its owner showed him where to mend
and repeated it. "I get yer meaning now,"
sighed Sam at the fourth or fifth attempt.

He made sure all of his repairs would last
so that he did not see the machine again.
At the forge, his bright red Irish eyebrows met
in puzzled furrows that filled up with sweat
while he hammered a new link for a chain
or struggled to weld a broken cast.

Horses were what he really understood
and all his shoes were even, firm and neat.
His father had been an army farrier;
on cold days the bewhiskered warrior
would leave the old men on the Townfoot seat
and hang about the smithy to warm his blood.

Tractors seemed invented for Sam's personal ruin,
but he could do nothing to prevent the horse
disappearing from the farms. His father,
who spoke some sense between heroic blethers,
took him back to Ireland and a racecourse
where he knew and liked what he was doing.

SADIE GILFILLAN
the Dairy Farmer

When Sadie's husband died, the town assumed
she would have to give up the dairy farm.
"If she thinks she can manage on her own,
there's no reason why she can't stay on,"
said Roderick Milne, to his factor's alarm.
"If she needs advice, you must give her some."

Sadie needed no advice. She knew
exactly how the dairy farm was run.
What she needed was some way to replace
her husband's long hours of work. Sadie faced
the problem and chose not to hire a man,
but to buy a milking machine and more cows.

She sold the old milk float and bought a van.
"She'll bankrupt herself," Gow the baker said,
but Sadie made a contract with the Co-op
for the surplus milk she could not bottle up.
She kept things simple, but her business head
knew better than stick to one rigid plan.

Sadie built hen batteries to her own design
and sold eggs. She had no time for sentiment.
Only once did the factor see her dark eyes blurred
with tears, when foot-and-mouth condemned her herd.
"Never you fear. I can still pay the rent,"
said Sadie as they covered up the lime.

WALTER SHAW
the Shepherd

Each year at the Strathinver Sheep Dog Trials
one shepherd towered above the others:
long Walter Shaw with his black-handled crook
and piercing eyes that were never meant for books
but for reading hillsides, burns and weather,
with a nose curved and sharp as a sundial.

Walter would put away his pipe and pouch,
wait till six ewes were let go on the Ben
and send off Roy and Nip in a wide sweep.
He'd whistle the dogs in behind the sheep
and keep them bunched until they reached the pen.
Walter, wide-open gate in hand, would crouch

till the sheep were almost in or call, "Haud up!"
if it looked as though young Nip would come too close
and make a nervous gimmer break away.
Then, stretching his long crook arm, he would say,
"In ye go," swing the gate and rope the post.
Year after year he won the shepherd's cup

and "best dog" medal. His knowledge of the scene
was needed one night when, in cold summer fog,
Jennie Milne was lost. Walter found her asleep,
snuggled in a corrie with some sheep.
He refused reward. "A new cup for best dog
at the trials?" said sly Milne. Walter's eyes gleamed.

ECK SKINNER
the Orraman

By the time Eck Skinner had reached twenty-one
he'd had eight employers all of whom agreed
that, even though he worked hard and meant well,
Eck was as safe as a bazooka shell.
Once at Leslie's farm he scythed some weeds,
went for his dinner and came back at one,

to meet Doctor Houston coming down the drive.
"Wha's no weel?" asked Eck. "Some idiot left a scythe
against a door and young John gashed his shin,"
said the doctor. Next week saw Eck begin
up at the Mains, but one day there he tried
to weigh the bull: "It's a wonder he's still alive."

Once Eck sat on a moving belt and was hurled
over a saw. He unblocked a diesel pump
"wi a guid sook." Only once he came to grief
when he fused the lights but kept on chopping neeps.
He lost two finger joints, gained a conundrum:
"Who's got the least rude V-sign in the world?"

SANDY AND MARTHA CRAIG
Tenant Farmers at Crossgate

Sandy Craig and his sister farmed Crossgate
and most of the year they managed all alone.
They kept cows and pigs, but very few,
and had no sheep. The main crop that they grew
was potatoes. The sowing work was done
with help from the Reid boys. Then they'd wait

till autumn settled on the yellow shaws.
They'd unlock the bothy, hope for no trouble,
then Nolans, MacAras, Raffertys and Boyles
would arrive in a green bus that dripped oil
and for three weeks the congregation would double
in Father Burke's bright, white-painted pews.

The repartee was quick. The work was slow,
and hindered by tinkering with the bus
that trundled them to and from the upturned drills.
They howked the tatties into crates and creels,
leaden-footed with mud or choked with dust
till five o'clock when Craig said, "That'll do."

The only part of the crime rate that would grow
was drunkenness, but while they were here
they took the blame for every fight or theft.
When the drills were empty and the old bus left
Craig would lock the bothy for another year,
glad to see them come, gladder to see them go.

BILLY GIBB
the Ploughman

In March the seagulls wheeled behind the plough
and in September tracked the binder's clatter,
swooping to pick up worms and fallen grain.
Billy Gibb would whirl his Fordie round again,
slam down his foot and make the seagulls scatter
as he lined up another dead-straight row.

All men and girls, except the shepherds, had to work
in the harvest fields. Billy set the pace
and a fast pace it was. The yellow stooks
were leaned like gossips or broth-tasting cooks.
Billy would work, while others ate their pieces
and only finished with the dew and dark.

He liked to work fast so he could show
the others that the army had been wrong
to turn him down because of his weak chest.
Madge Todd was the only one he impressed
but their stubble-stiff romance survived as long
as the brittle favour of a harvest bow.

JOHN LESLIE
Tenant Farmer of Muirhead Farm

John Leslie, when he reached eighty, retired
and exchanged houses with his son, young John
who moved to the farmhouse while the old man went
to Muirhead cottage, with the Milnes' consent
and a silver tray inscribed by everyone
on the farm. His grandsons built a huge bonfire;

tradition began it for old John;
then folk said, "It's for the Coronation."
Everest news of Hillary and Tensing
meant that the bonfire should mark everything
that might be the cause of celebration.
All through May, until the Second of June

it grew from old planks, brushwood, burst tyres, spars
dragged up by hand to the top of the Ben.
Blackout curtains, gasmasks went into it,
anything old and dark that could be lit.
It blazed for John, for Tensing and the Queen
and to drive out the last shadows of the war.